ESTRANGEMENTS

Also by Arthur Freeman · Apollonian Poems

Estrangements

Arthur Freeman

HARCOURT, BRACE & WORLD, INC. · NEW YORK

First edition

Library of Congress Catalog Card Number: 66-15016
Printed in the United States of America

The poem "Naples Again" appeared originally in *The New Yorker*; "Beauty, Sleeping," "The Occupation," and a version of "Troilus and Company" in *Poetry*. Other poems were first published in *The American Scholar*, *The Atlantic Monthly*, *Identity Magazine*, *Three-Penny Papers*, the New York *Times*, and the *William & Mary Review*.

J. L. H.

CONTENTS

Part I

Part II

Part III

I

I

THE DOG FAR HENCE

If, at midmorning on the bayside beach
when the tide lays out its nets of trash and gravel,
you chance on that transparent skeletal fish
propped among the pebbles, its grin and eyes
peopled with flies,
cartilage only, but not quite
past stinking—cover it up—but no use piling
black slats and wreckage under the wet sand,
no use the beercans or the scattered chips
of ships
all over it, as nevertheless
some long-maned lion of a dog like that
over there—friendly, shaggy, dumb—
will disinter the mess and bear it home
like a tributary bone
back to the mispleased master, who, like you,
carried away no living or dead thing
from the contaminate display
but only stones, perhaps, or glass, or a shell
which didn't smell.

DRINK ME

There everything is warm, even the whiskey,
like a doll's house with a painted hearth
where Jack and Jill sit woodenly
in the sitting room by the Set,

the small house round which cold and dark
ring down their curtains at six
and the ice inevitably runs out
at nine, while the glass mask blinks
and stammers like a court of law,
where we sit with our faces lit by it
with our pocketed hands
and our heads screwed on one way.

Whole hours slip though our grip here
like ice, and the ashtrays fill up and spill.
Only the mismatched drapes won't quite
lap over, and our bottled light
leaks out into the street—
but for the time, at nightfall,
I am a toy with a toy wife taking place
where everything is warm, dollhouse and dishes,
pillows and drinks and firelight on the cat
from the imaginary grate.

The tight bright house that cradles us
with our woolen heads and no voices

nor a wolf at the windy screendoor—
                              listen, I think
I have swallowed the wrong warm drink, and overgrown
all of it, matchsticks, thatch, and lacquer,
shouldered the roof and laid low the walls
while the rain pours in and the lamps go out
and I only and my clumsiness remain now
in the unapologizing dark. Good night.

The cicadas in the fir-grove drone a hum-drum
unremitting kind of chorus to the climate,
and the pre-Socratic sun suggests its questions,
and the sky remains as empty and as bright

and unanswering as ever, since it opened,
mute and blue, on the earliest of mornings;
while in Daphni there is only sun and stoneware
and a wilderness as barren as the past.

Let the sterner Pantocrater shadow lightning;
let the milder Christs wear mercy in their alcoves;
still the springs choke, and the images still moulder,
and at Daphni is indifference at the last.

INTERIOR

Moving among the familiar furniture of her love
once more in the accustomed house, her home,
he, like a lifelong but exploratory guest
tested his welcome with his eyes—as if
the questions offered her were flowers
of her own, and of her choice; and she,
knowing the words already, and the moves
and all the meanings and expected answers,
once, because no grace is perfectly
hospitable, let slip her smile
                              like a breakable vase
which he caught deftly, stooping, as
the anticipation of a crash
heightened the silence; and he gave it back
intact, with a reproof to her,
who accepted it gravely, fitted the flowers into place,
and held it now like an acknowledgment
of thanks—for everything. Observe
upon the mantel now, their
tenuous bouquet.

NEGATIVE CAPABILITY

There is in union itself
an ultimate frustration
that a distinguished *two* can come
no closer than becoming *one*.

Nothing sublimer than sublime—
No pleasures beyond ecstasies—
as ultimates contain extremes
so unions proximities.

O unimaginative sphere
where consummations burn their bridges!
I am afraid, still, of such fire.
I require surfaces and edges.

For I love you and don't love Love.
Better I say to hang uncertain
upon some pitch, be tentative,
grappling for balance and possession,

than let slip all the homing passions.
Passion would spend what Love accrued,
and in a blaze of brittle unions
apocalyptically conclude.

WHAT IT WAS

What was it, if not pride, that racked my heart
when, with less bitterness than I descried,
you loosed us both? Not love, I said, but pride,
pride mortified, surely, that took the part

of love undone, and pride that made me smart.
Pain made me wiser, whereby I discerned
what love was, what self-love was, and I learned
what it was, if not pride, that racked my heart.

AUTUMNAL

The knowledgeable geese have fled.
The sun is cold now and oblique.
The leaves beneath the trees are dead.

The clear air tightens like a fist,
and blades of grass go singly stiff
in separate focuses of frost.

The air's so clear you draw your breath
in pain at last. Cold certainty
dilates the heart; and it is Death

whistling for wind that you have heard.
Now do your reveries of Heaven
scatter everywhere like birds?

WHAT IS UNWOVEN

Never, though sky from sky divide by night,
and sea, beneath the prow, relinquish sea,
though star with starfall part, and perish light,
never so casually shall we.

Nor though the senseless particles of stone
diversify to dust, and rest apart,
and frailty corrupting flesh and bone
dissolve all but the heart,

though dark chagrin accumulate like tears,
and bitterness like wind behind the sky,
though reason lift the mist, and tell our years,
we shall not wholly comply.

Yet we shall part; we know it, and know why.
As every element knows bliss and bane,
we know our pain and pleasure; as the sky
divides by gentlest rain

we shall divide. Dearest, but as the sea
makes one once more behind the parting prow,
memory, like a wake, must bind and weave
what is unwoven now.

TROILUS AND COMPANY

What a pair we are, I swear. Who would admit
—given this vogue of rough-hewn honesty—
half the shellacked hypocrisy we've split?
Magnificent almost, it seems to me,
how false we play ourselves, what piquancy
peppers our trumped-up quarrels, and what wit
the casuist oaths we opt! Come lovers, grit
your gums, and elders, crack a smile: it's we.

Sometimes, however, it becomes a bore.
After this script has hedged and hemmed and hawed
I even slip: I'd call a fraud a fraud
and fault the times, the mores, and The War,
cast flesh the villain, nature for the bawd,
and *lupus in fabula* who's back for more.

BEAUTY, SLEEPING

My mistress' inmost heart,
how does it keep so deep
that neither sentiment nor art
   can sound its sleep?

Where does this dreamer lie
when the prince rides round the camp?
Up in some tower, high and dry,
   or deep and damp?

Is it a citadel
he must perforce assail,
or is it woods, or might he as well
   begin in jail?

And when he knows, then what?
Suppose there is a lock,
and the last doors are bolted shut—
   shall he knock?

Grant him a miracle.
Admit him to the place,
and let him bend to break the spell,
   facing her face,

And then, ironic Three,
administer your pill—

let him embrace her perfectly
and her sleep still.

Oh mistress mine, I fear
I seek who shall refuse me.
You who are difficult and dear—
excuse me.

SONG AFTER A BAD NIGHT

To be old, and sick of pleasure, and incapable of harming,
to sleep dreamlessly, want nothing but repose and a slow fire,
what a providential prospect! Undemanding, unalarming,
in a coffin of self-knowledge in a vacuum of desire.

All mixed motives disentangled, love and pity, hurt and hate,
graded, named, and segregated, limp and chill as wickered bait,
with no afterthought extruding like a live claw from its sty,
and no impulse hoarded in the heart's crust to survive and
    ramify.

O what invalided bliss! I am tired of being clever.
I'm a failure as a sleeper, I'm a loafer of a lover,
I'm a quay without a loch to line, a lake is in my liver—
to be old, and sick, and harmless; to be hopeless; to be over.

FOR A LIMITED TIME ONLY

Twice a day even the sea knocks off
persecuting the same headland,
gnawing the highwater rocks
with its weed teeth, and withdraws.
My heart shifts its burdens.

II

REVISITED

The cold stone wall of windows as before,
the same split tiles, the sunlight darkening
varnish on a renovated door
over which the same caged canaries sing.
Shopfronts alone pay change: the shabby turn
chic, the old names fall, the old awnings burn.

Prices go up, we think, and the parks seem
smaller perhaps—we can accept small change—
but with the unaffected it is we
who alter, and by altering estrange:
spires that no longer draw our eyes, and if
the familiar cathedral is no less itself

we are the less; if what was once for us
in a nave's depth unfathomable light
resolves now to sunshine through colored glass,
our eyes are dimmer, and our appetite
duller by tasting. Custom has blunted it.
Only the unconsummated visit

finally in the mind perpetuates
its piquancy, like a last chance intact.
Memory cannot bleach it, retrospect
exhaust it, or comparison degrade
what is imaginary, absent, and austere
as the aloof moon in the sunlit air.

WEEDS

Wrong, certainly, to grasp it by the stalk
or the distinguishing foliage, and pull—
always the rubbery roots break halfway off.
The middle one in particular,
the spine, snaps every time: ease it up
tenderly from the base, like a trout-bone,
because if anything remains below
the whole weed flowers up again like new.

It's so much trouble, God knows I am sick
of it, poetry, with its breakable back,
nursing along each line with those stray words
that pop off, and the rhymes that stick. Somewhere
there has to be a natural estate
of raw ideas sans husbandry in leaf
with buried meanings, in a complete field
undivoted by art. Meanwhile, this patch.

MOTHS

Watered-silk wings beat wildly, ten frail flaps
each inch of elevation from the lawn,
hefting the unflightworthy thoraxes, which fail,
and rise, and fail again. One rigorous minute's
random frenzy, and they've flown
a shrub's height, whence they parachute to pose
stiffbacked a jittery moment, and resume.
At rest, the rich blue figured wings clap shut
like doublures dustless in a shelved Derôme:
and only *in vitro* may we trace the veined
black lapis of their wasted beauty, spreadeagled
by ether, pricked to glass. Whereas now haste
compels them. The sun goose-steps to noon.

Restiveness closes the notebook; unconstrained,
a fagged attention flaps toward lunch: why waste
my little patience and short shopworn hours
on paradigms pat as moths? Some days
when the world's burning, fiddling makes it worse.
Conscience, you'll have to nail me to my verse.

ÉMIGRÉ

The patched-together violin
melts with its melody like gum,
and the guitar alongside him
like any nameless alien
filling a form, numbly, replies.
His transient's smile, his exiled eyes
that wander on the shadowed walls
make do with a lean memory
of words, and what the wrist recalls,
aimless as pensioners. Off key
at last, the discord brings him back
to the irreparable wreck
of frayed strings and cracked ebony
and no more art. He'll pass the plate.
Poor old regime, poor delegate
of a dead age, a dead way,
telling the same old tales for pay
whose words, like cancelled papers, catch
in his throat, that strictest *douanier*.
His lips close on them like a latch.

CUT LAURELS

Among the last acts of the lady in the park
whose face is crumpled as a cabbage, and whose pinched eyes
glint like oysters in the settling dark,
has been in perfect silence to have gazed

past the unpardonable children churning turf,
the lovers tangled on the benches, the brisk prams
and chipper nannies, to the tarnished rump
of the benign brass stallion of a king of France

for thirty minutes; for three hundred years
rider and horse have seemed about to part,
such pedestalled impatience paws the air.
But execution is the tease of art,

and rather, the old lady it will be,
shouldering her sackcloth, who must rise,
resigned to living, and lag home to sleep
and die, as, ultimately, you and I.

THE CELL OF HIMSELF

"Fermons nos coeurs à double tour"

In the middle of the night in the next room
a man who is no friend of mine cries out,
struggling with sleep; it is a nightmare.
It is not my nightmare. We share nothing
but the awareness of each other through one wall,
the groan of a drain, an occasional involuntary
outcry, and no more. We want no more.
We could be happier with less.

And there are others like us, billeted
all over the impartial city
in similar honeycombs at the same rates,
keeping apart for the particular reason
that no reason binds us, silhouettes
of habit, ghosts of motion. Nothing remains
of what is laudable in each but noise
to alien ears which value absence best.

And ultimately more who have cast off
proximity like mooring, and float free
of the contiguities we suffer by.
Wax in a window may consume itself
for them, but they are admirably gone,
past echo and sight; and if the piled
horizon whitens them no unbroached shores,
sea will suffice, and they will bear with sea.

And I would have it no way else: no smile
extracted on the stair, no hesitant
exchange, no names. Drains are enough.
The intimacy each man may cultivate
with his own cloudy mirror does for me,
and when that image grates on the dry sight,
let me acquaint myself with anyone
but this, whose dreamt fright arrogates my sleep.

Now it is four, my clock walks heavily.
I hear him settling, reassured, to rest,
with a clear mind and a diminished pulse.
But I lie now wide-eyed in the grey light
continuing his dream like a disease
my mind made welcome when his cast it out.
My cry caught in my throat, while the thin walls
thicken like distance, I am most alone.

AT THE SAME TIME

Shadows cover the locked park like awe;
the lilacs instantly hold still.
A block off it is Saturday traffic,
but the blackbirds forage on short grass
and the willows droop here without waiting.
Simultaneously elsewhere a multitude
tramples everything with unflagging energy,
and the city shifts like mud in its bed,
the farting buses rut up the roads,
the lights snap on and off permission
and the revolving doors issue like meat grinders.
My pitiful artificially native park
gathers the free breezes of the square, gathers silence,
darkens, preens, and holds perfectly
still, finally, while the unhappy
warlords of redevelopment go on fixing it
in their intentional bombsites like a dream of home.

MARCH

The appletrees webbed with snow in the warm morning,
sunlit, sugary, brittle as coral
when the laced boughs brush against wind,
shower powder like rice,
and the sheet ice rifts
and floods over choked falls. By noon
grass seams the snow, rocks pit and patch it,
and green islands of reeds lean with the stream
until there is mud everywhere. Tonight
pigs dance in the yard—
moonlit like marble their sleek bodies
loping, slow, stately, their clumsiness
musical, deepvoiced and molten, in uncovered earth.

Magnificent roistering animals
in their own sweet season, they embrace
in the moistest mud—an unmixed blessing
for the hoofed and unshod,
who snuffle among these naked apples, heedlessly
hedonistic, for the unbegun fruit.

COMPANY

On the wet black street tire tracks
like stripped adhesive twist and cross
and braid where the cars weave themselves
to a standstill. Rain on my window
threads down the glass by drops
at snail's pace with a snail's zigzags
and the slick paths come together and blot
and begin again. I am tracing out
patterns in steam settled
on the inside of the window, thinking of how
minds meet, and bodies bind,
and the single lives that hew lines
singly, marry at last their own slow flow.

GONE

The lame iron table under the awning, and the empty glass
with its vaporous tracery of Export, laid exposed
in an unrelieved armistice of noon,
where the air itself seems empty, and the wind
suspended, the streets silent and dry,
speak for the absences we alter by—
sight out of mind, ours, others', finally
an unabashed unblinking vacancy
of spirit, when the customary past
misses its niche in a razed consciousness,
and the memory shakes in its own dazzling light.
Back of a sunstruck and unshaded eye
love and the lost loved ones bubble off
like froth in a forgotten vessel, left
out elsewhere, in a place without a wind,
empty at present, but where crowds have been.

III

LAND'S END: POINTE DU RAZ

The south wind harries the rain broadside to the point.
Eddying slips, blue luminous whorls, the rock sharks'-teeth
curdling a scrap of caught water to the lee,
while on the windward face, unharnessed headlong
hosts of choke-tide sea break on the spit,
a bodiless animus borne to its bleak end—

but bleaker the high grizzly water, sharper
the waves' teeth, the frozen anguish of assault
that tasks this coiled force to its visceral resorts.
To plunge, to prise into the heart of hate!
To taste its adamant design, harsh brine,
tyrannical thrash, the steel of its intransigeance

icing the veins, to bear its singleness
in a burst body to the nether beach!
Guidelines of buried peaks blaze to the calm
recesses of past deep, where drownèd Ys
lies, and the long locks of *la belle Dahut*
weave among fish—fair, false, and twice betrayed,

poor wicked princess, cast off by the good—
shall we seek out that city of wide eyes,
still hearts, cursed beauty, and kept peace? Or flee
like the good Gradlon, thrusting from his back
the incubus of love—and live, at last bestrid
by sanctity, to an exampled age?

Sink rather, sink with Ys, in tackles knit
of the fair hair of myth, to where
no change nor choice can rack what is composed.
Passion and pain may harrow the wide world,
but there, eaved in the eye of violence,
that shadowy valley swims in speculation.

Ultimate quietude, ultimate ease,
world without mutability or loss,
what vistas there would yawn beneath your wish,
could act admit. Wave upon wave commits
its agony to the unyielding rock.
O paragon of constancy, the will is weak!

Wind blinds the naked eye, as rain the glass,
and faltering, the spirit shrinks from faith:
witness the tempest's Terror, limp split limbs
of pine dangling like noosed men miles inland,
starved thatch, flayed patience, the main unappeased—
shoulder this Devil's weather and go in.

But when the wind lifts, and the rain draws west,
and from a packed reorienting sky
light, like a slow custodian's contempt,
returns, ask of your eyes: *Dites*, what was seen?
The land jostling the sea, as dreaming, death;
a glimpse—when hesitancy blinkered you—

sensed only, unperceived? What we have closed
our lashed lids to, will sleep expose?
In stillness sunlight crackles on the foam,

scaling those surfaces hard gilded green
and glassy blue, whereto the staggered pairs
of isolated peaks descend like stairs.

Gradlon was the virtuous sixth-century king of Ys, a legendary
city on the coast of Western Brittany, supposed the most
exquisite in the world. His beloved daughter, beautiful but
depraved Dahut, was persuaded by the devil in the guise of a
handsome young man to unlock the gates of the wall which
protected Ys from the sea. While her father slept, Dahut stole
his keys and accomplished this; whereupon the sea swept in and
inundated the city. Gradlon caught up his daughter and
attempted to escape on horseback to higher ground, but the
sea pursued him inland, and at last a celestial voice directed
him, for his own preservation, to "cast off the devil that rides
behind you." Cradlon obeyed and survived, and went on, with
the spiritual aid of a Breton saint, Corentin, to found a new
city—present day Quimper—and died many years afterward in
an odor of holiness. Ys and its inhabitants, we are told, will
rise from the sea on the Day of Judgement; and in the mean-
time Dahut has become a siren who lures sailors to shipwreck on
the dangerous rocks which line the coast north and south of
Pointe du Raz.

DARK GLASSES: VENICE

A polarized moon at noon in the matte sky
casts its paralysis all over the piazza.
The pastels drain and fuse, the gilding
on the imperial ensigns washes white,
and July's botched mosaic of pan-national faces
in the buzzing sun wanes away
to one harmless homogeny, chewing-gum-colored.
Pigeons, hawks, and municipal griffins
appear the same glareless grey.

And the shadow lines vanish, the hobbling pulse
halts, steadies itself, the retinas stop smarting.
Voices, graceless gutturals and jackhammer Latin,
blur and blend, and the news in the newspaper darkens
brown as last century's. Dark glasses did it.
Dark glasses smug in their own shade say
peace, simplicity, silence, and beauty
are better than people: oh, anything to anaesthetize
that stintless sunbeat drumming the rotten conscience
et in Bogalusa ego,
ego, ego, ego, like a cracked record, echoing.

THE OCCUPATION

I

Arrowy firs procession
a nagging slow line of olive camions
with funereal headlamps
on the road rolling up low hills.
A sunset's staccato
spits between worn-out outbuildings,
and shorn meadows diminish into flats.
By night, in sullen towns,
a counterattack of eyes with the exact change: _Danke._

Our white headlights
rake empty earth as we wind
home to a landmined courtesy,
political ease, the smooth steel of _entente_,
where memory like a barbed frontier
contains each gesture: _Bitte._

No rest for the watchful, you and I
who bivouacked
in all that hostile and pervading air.
What rubbed off? Anger,
welled in the stagnant heart, draws out
its venom in each artery.
What's mine is yours. _Ich liebe dich._

II: Munich by Night

Puff paste and cinnamon: cupolas
and candy bow-bells, the lit lanes,
gemmed and crystalline vitrines,
bloom like bewitched woods in the way

where one or two trail unbelief.
A distant music sugars
the brown evening, as all thumb-faced burghers
shoulder their axes and knock off

for ninepins in the dell. Dreaming:
this meerschaum and tobacco chapel's
unshelled face and silver bells
chime, changelessly disarming,

and the elves throw down their plowshares,
the old sorceress her hexes,
even the werewolves backtrack
and the cake house cracks, when there appears

Sir Percival from Paradise.
See how he rides, on a high horse
caparisoned in light, like promise—
Prosit! The city scours its eyes

and rises to the appetite.
While *Alma Mater über Alles*
rings from the busy beerhalls
all the disenchanted night

unanimous as laughter,
crying, Up the Prototype,
Pied Percivals in jackboots pipe
their faithful to Forever After.

III

Herr *Ach* preferred Americans.
Russians, the whole world knows, are truculent,
pigheaded, and plain dull

as predictable instructions.
Unwilling to dicker,
they had locked him up,

in that paradise prime
for the plucking, while *they* toed the line—
then, of all times,

when fortunes fell to the touch
like overripe peaches
in hijacked tobacco,

petrol, chocolate,
rock-bottom real estate
for the long range

and morphine for the short.
Only to know what's what
and above all, languages

like Herr *Ach*—whose English
prefers him as he prefers it
even now as before, although nothing

is easy—and tally the revenue.
Obstinate, obstinate Ivans!
—Praise God, it was better with you,

and why not? We are realists,
we, for whom warring is childish,
revenge sentimental,

resentment, which cripples the heart
and unsteadies the target,
profitless. Look:

if you travel to England
pack gold from Geneva.
This card is my friend's,

advised *Ach*, with a flash
of *echt* comradely cunning,
inclining goodbye—Demand cash.

IV

All winter the brittle windows of our house
framed angular landscapes of black earth
and snow-white space above the apple-trees
jacketed with ice. We closed off all but two rooms
while one thirsty burner drained jerrycans
of rationed oil on coupons spared us
by the next-door draftee and his bride,
both nineteen, with a year-old child, dirt poor.
In hospital, losing her second,
she pored through magazines from the PX—
Teen-Age Romance, Young Marriage, Photoplay.
And he at home, too young to drink,
mooned over movies and mail, and the cold shoulders
of shopgirls, till the Army shipped back both.

Cold March in that fishbowl of a house
where strange fowl clucked in the eaves
and the landlord and his pitchfork wore a path
between the barn and pigsty nightly
without knocking. A stolid rain
began in April and persisted
until shoals of mud encompassed the lone rock
we tenanted. The farmer vanished.
Only the whistling pigeons lasted
beneath the soaking drip in the dry eaves
honing our nerves. Alien spring
misted its windows like a flush
of choked-back petulance, and in our fields
unbending wheatblades skewered the moist soil
where thrift and solitude had sown their teeth.

V: Chess

Teaching the elements, from Capablanca,
I embody that master's patience
as principles, clear as water, flower
from the old figures. Follow him
where inexorable style
may execute what the impersonal intent
designed, in the exacting space,
by the still logic of pursuit, counterthrust,
harmony of sacrifice and gain,
the *Realpolitik* of play—
                    Whereas you make of it
a wilderness of motivated shapes
where, in the alternating light,
impassable alleys and diagonals extend
from the blunt rook and visored bishop
to the fastness of the hobbled crown,
where unpredictably white knights wheel
and the black pawns mesh like teeth. Each piece
an idiosyncrasy, each for itself,
personal as damned angels
in a limbo of mistakes. You see
what veils the game,
what labels agents of pure force
beatitudes and devils, as a child
makes pagan his domain by naming parts.
Chess, chess is simpler—black and white
in a closed quarter, undemanding,

unrevealing, meaningless
but by analogy:
             You have seen
those roundheads marshal in the city squares
fulfilling patterns they know nothing of
for visored masters; and the taken men
can be replaced, and the game played again.

VI

—If you simply would wipe the tub
with the sponge stuffed in the trap
of the sink, specifically for that purpose,
not with a washcloth or a towel—
And screw the cap back on the toothpaste,
please? It's a reminder
of my broken home. Now, ashes
everywhere but in the ashtrays,
I can't stand it, it's so much like—
Must you wear short socks? Your dandruff,
worse? I know you don't like leeks, but try
this once, I'm sure you'll learn.
We'll need more coupons soon, God knows
where we can find them, perhaps you—
Don't drum with your fingers. Please don't hum—
Do something! Something new!

—Nothing is new. Anyway, it's raining.

VII

The plane pants to its hangar
in Boston, this Fourth-of-July, near noon.
Blistering heat beats on the fuselage,
white light, still air
smelling of peanut shells and piss.
Like dazzled owls we hesitate
at the top of the gangway. Coming down
gingerly upon soft macadam,
with a taut flight-bag and five fifths,
to a confetti of faces
at the barrier—home, as they say,

with my rubble in two suitcases,
the last yards of the fare drained dry.
By common choice you stay,
wherefore the sun's red pendulum ticked six
jet hours from vanished Cause
to these effects:

Quarrelsome tile against the step,
steel harsh to the hand,
splinters of neon, rock on the p.a.
I buy a paper with my lucky dime:
Goldwater on page one,

his palpable teeth picketing
the public smile, his coal eyes feathered
silver and black, like wrapped arrows.

Fjords of print chill each cliché; each word
blisters the silver brow. There's hate,
hate in the papers, in the pulse,
pride's manners, and one white unsettling face
like the moon's above subdued mills,
bland, risen, the fat fruit of thinking so . . .

My charity lies bleeding in its glow.

NAPLES AGAIN

The hills yet hills, and still the yellow town
declines into the sea by particles.
Six years: so many grams of dust dispersed,
so many repetitions of the sky,
so many skins of spring sloughed off, and snows
melted, to move the dial of days
to February of a similar year,
myself to the same stance and place.

By the long bay I walked, where fishermen
of Mergellina thrash their crusted nets
in shallow water to shake loose the mud.
Where the balloonman piped, and the slow sea
smothered a colony of rocks with weeds
—abundant, rust-colored, and rank—
patterns of change and sameness filmed my mind
like oilslick in the pitted bank.

Six years, what have I never learned—like silt
to shake free or be shaken in good time?
Like the high, unaccommodating rock
to bear with dignity the yoke of grass?
Even the salt wash whispers in reproach:
see how insinuation speeds
my lightness to the limit of the beach,
beyond the rocks, beyond the weeds.

*

Here then the unsought accidence of place
and the false glass of nature warp me. Hills
borrow the furled brows of the lately dead,
the sky the wide eyes of the living. Bent
by the conviction of analogy,
the credulousness of a dumb thing,
the tired mind buckles and the stripped will
relaxes its questioning.

See with what unconcern the tides demesne
each to its niche: crayfish and pebble, shells
by the unshelled, and chip by parent block—
such as it is, the natural effect,
the disposition of all patiently
predictable as the sea,
undifferentiated, dumb. Silt, stones, and froth—
am I and all things more than these?

But the wind's wisdom comes too easy now,
and reason wriggles on its string like bait,
and again life is more than metaphor.
Up on the hill the starved and savage cats
swallow their nature to take milk at hand
and wail all night to charm it back.
Haphazard children in the shadowed slums
torture their narrow eyes with chalk

and beg in the great squares; and some men pay
and some will not; and there is no design.
I and the waterfront must draft our peace

if what I learn is not what the earth learns,
if what I doubt is all my discipline;
for earth persists, and in good time
—when I am the same silent element—
may set its simpler meaning over mine.